The Coral Reef

Written by Sarah O'Neil

Series Consultant: Linda Hoyt

WorldWise™
Content-based Learning

T0359544

Contents

Chapter 1

The coral reef

If you go **snorkelling** or **scuba** diving around many islands in the **tropical** regions of the world, you will come across amazing underwater structures. These structures are coral reefs.

Coral reefs contain hundreds of different types of coral and are home to thousands of sea creatures. All these living things have developed amazing behaviours to survive. Coral reefs are some of the most complex **habitats** on Earth.

Yet despite their size, coral reefs are **fragile** environments that are easily damaged by the things that people do. Many coral reefs have been made into **marine parks** where there are rules about what people cannot do.

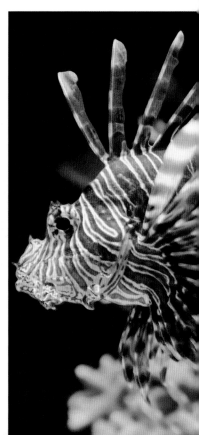

Did you know?

The largest coral reef in the world is the Great Barrier Reef. It is found along the east coast of Australia. It is made up of more than 2,900 individual reefs and over 900 islands.

Anthias

A lionfish swims on the reef.

Sea slug

Coral reefs: A special ecosystem

Coral reefs can be found along the coast of over 100 countries. Although they are the habitat for a huge number of **marine** plants and animals, they cover less than one percent of the ocean floor. This is because coral reefs are made by living things that can grow only in certain conditions.

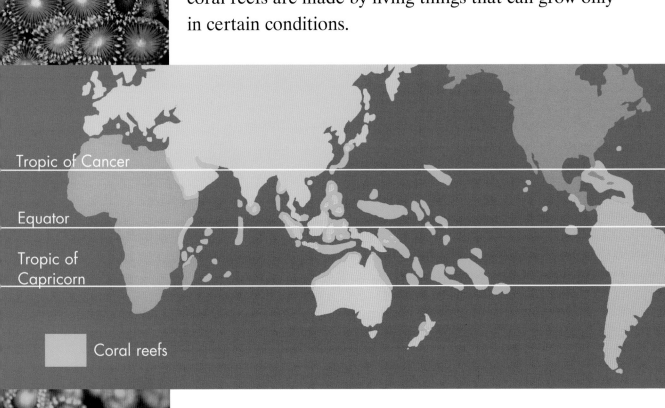

Tropic of Cancer

Equator

Tropic of Capricorn

Coral reefs

Coral reefs are made up of huge numbers of tiny coral **polyps**. Even though coral polyps look like plants, they are actually animals.

Coral polyps have **algae** living in their bodies. Like plants, these algae can make food from sunlight. Coral polyps eat some of the food made by the algae. This lets the coral grow up to three times faster than they could without the algae.

Coral polyps

What conditions do coral polyps need?

Coral polyps need to grow in shallow water so they can get plenty of sunlight. Sunlight allows the algae that live inside the polyps to make food.

Coral needs clean water because the polyps are easily damaged or killed by dirty water. Pollution is a major threat to coral reefs.

Coral needs clear water. If there is too much dirt or plankton in the water, the algae in coral polyps don't get enough sunlight to make food.

Reef-building coral can live only in water that is a certain temperature. If the water gets too hot or too cold, the coral will die. When this happens, it is called coral bleaching.

Coral needs salty water. Like many sea animals, the polyps cannot live in fresh water. They do not grow near river mouths, because of the fresh water coming from the river.

7

Chapter 2

Questions about coral

Sarah is a marine biologist. She studies the sea and the plants and animals that live in it. As part of her job she answers questions about the coral reef.

Q. What are coral reefs?

A. Coral reefs are huge rocky structures made out of limestone. They form a **marine habitat** that supports a huge amount of the ocean's wildlife. About a quarter of all life in the sea relies on coral reefs.

Did you know?

Coral polyps are in the same family as sea anemones. They are also related to jellyfish.

A coral reef

8

Q. Where does the limestone come from?

A. The limestone in coral reefs is made from the skeletons of coral **polyps**. Coral polyps live together in huge **colonies**. When coral polyps die, their skeletons remain. This makes up the non-living structure of the reef. Living polyps grow on top of the skeletons. When they die, their skeletons will be left behind too. The reef slowly grows towards the sun in this way.

Did you know?
When people talk about coral they are referring to both the animals and the skeletons coral polyps leave behind when they die.

Stony coral with open polyps

Q. Do all coral polyps help to build the reef?
A. No. There are many different kinds of coral, but most can be classified as hard or soft coral. Only hard coral polyps leave behind limestone skeletons when they die. Soft coral polyps don't have hard skeletons, so they do not build reefs.

Q. What colour are coral polyps?
A. Most coral polyps have clear bodies and white skeletons. Most coral polyps get their amazing colours from **algae** that live inside their bodies.

Soft coral

Hard coral

Q. What do coral polyps eat?
A. Coral polyps eat some of the food made by the algae that live inside their bodies. They also feed on **microscopic** animals that live in the water, called **zooplankton**.

Q. Can coral polyps move?
A. No. Coral polyps rely on ocean **currents** to bring them food and to take away their wastes. Many corals also rely on currents to reproduce and to take their young to a new place where they can settle and grow. This is the way new coral reefs are formed.

Zooplankton, the microscopic animals that coral polyps eat.

?

Did you know?
The staghorn coral is the fastest-growing coral. It can grow up to as much as 30 centimetres a year. Slower growing coral grows about 4 millimetres a year.

Chapter 3

Life on a coral reef

Scientists estimate that coral reefs support as wide a range of living things as rainforests do on the land. Millions of fish and other sea creatures rely on the coral reef for food and shelter. Some of its **inhabitants** are awake during the day and rest at night; others rest during the day and are active at night. Some creatures live on the reef all the time; others just visit.

Animals of the coral reef

The Christmas tree worm uses its arms to **sieve** or sift food from the water. If it senses danger it quickly shrinks back into the coral.

Giant clams attach themselves to the reef. They eat tiny animals and plants they sift from the water.

Sea turtles visit the reef looking for food. Sandy islands formed by the reef provide safe places where the female turtles can lay their eggs.

Tiger sharks are **scavengers** that visit coral reefs looking for food. They eat the dead animals that they find.

| Day | Night |

Throughout the day, coral **polyps** are usually inactive with their tentacles withdrawn. But the **algae** that live inside them are awake and making food from sunlight.

Most coral come out at night. They extend stinging tentacles to catch **zooplankton**, which float past on the **current**.

| Day | Night |

Parrot fish bite coral with their beak-like mouths to eat the algae that grows in it. The hard part of the coral is excreted as sand. Parrot fish produce most of the sand that is found around coral reefs.

To stay safe at night, parrot fish make a bubble of slime all over themselves. Scientists think the slime bubble may stop predators from finding the parrot fish by smell.

| Day | Night |

Reef sharks are inactive during the day. They rest in caves or on the bottom of the ocean.

Reef sharks hunt in the dark. They find food using their ability to sense the small amounts of electricity animals give off.

The food web

Lots of animals live on coral reefs because it is a place where food is plentiful. In the warm climate where coral thrives, many plants and algae can grow. This means that many plant-eating animals can live there. Meat-eating animals come to eat the plant eaters. This forms a food web.

Think about ...
What would happen to the coral reef if all the algae died?

The food web on a coral reef

means "is eaten by"

reef shark

parrot fish

octopus

trigger fish

coral polyp

crab

sea urchin

zooplankton

seagrass

algae

plant plankton

Living together

Many of the living things that make their home on a coral reef work together to survive. They can help each other find food and stay clean, or they can keep each other safe. When creatures of different species cooperate like this, it is called a symbiotic relationship. Coral polyps have a symbiotic relationship with algae. The following chart explains some other symbiotic relationships.

Animals need to keep their bodies clean.

This is very difficult for fish to do by themselves. Some fish have a relationship with shrimp that solves this problem. Cleaner shrimp get food by cleaning the skin of much bigger fish. Normally, big fish would eat shrimp. But the fish being cleaned stays still while the cleaner shrimp nibbles off the dirt and parasites. The cleaner shrimp get food while the fish are cleaned.

Clown fish and anemones also work together.

Anemones have stinging tentacles that paralyse any fish that it touches. But clown fish have a coating of protective slime that stops anemones from hurting them. A clown fish will swim through an anemone's tentacles, attracting fish that prey on clown fish. Then the anemone can catch the other fish, which keeps the clown fish safe. Clown fish also eat scraps of food not eaten by the anemones.

Some jellyfish and algae have a symbiotic relationship.

The algae live in the jellyfish and make food from sunlight. The jellyfish eats some of this food. The jellyfish swims close to the surface of the water, which lets the algae get a lot of sunlight.

Some small fish have symbiotic relationships with bigger fish.

Like cleaner shrimp, the cleaner fish eat the parasites off the bodies of bigger fish.

The octopus: A case study

The octopus is a fascinating animal. There are more than 150 different kinds of octopuses. They are found in many places in the ocean, including the coral reef.

Octopuses are in the same animal family as squid, cuttlefish, mussels, clams and snails. They lay eggs on the ocean floor, where they live. Many octopuses make dens in small cracks or caves. Octopuses rest, hide from predators and wait for prey to come near in these dens.

Octopuses eat crabs, clams, lobsters, snails, fish and even other octopuses. They usually hunt during the night.

Octopuses have saliva that dissolves the bodies of their prey to make it easier to eat. They also have a beak-like mouth they use to bite into the hard shells that some of their prey have.

18

Octopuses don't have any bones in their soft bodies. This means they can slip though very small cracks to escape predators. Octopuses have eight arms called tentacles. They can regrow a tentacle if they lose one. Each tentacle has two rows of suckers and receptors that can detect the movement of prey.

Octopuses can move fast. They can pull themselves with their tentacles, or push themselves rapidly through the water by taking in water and then squirting it out of their siphon-like mouths. A medium-sized octopus can travel at 13 kilometres per hour jetting backwards.

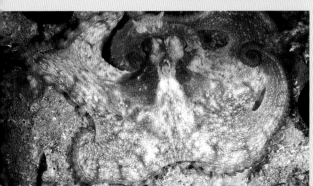

Octopuses are good at camouflage. They change colour to blend in with their surroundings. Some octopuses can change the texture of their skin, and some even make themselves look like poisonous sea creatures such as sea snakes to trick predators.

Octopuses can also hide themselves by squirting out a cloud of ink. This confuses predators and makes it easier for the octopus to escape.

Did you know?
The biggest octopus is the giant octopus. It can measure seven metres long. The smallest octopus is the Californian octopus. It is only one centimetre long.

Chapter 4

Reef under threat!

Although coral reefs are big, they are **fragile** and easily damaged by climate change and pollution.

Climate change causes the seawater around coral reefs to warm, which can cause coral bleaching. Once coral bleaching occurs, the coral reef may never regrow. This has already happened in many places.

Pollution also damages coral reefs. If the water around coral reefs gets contaminated with chemicals or waste, the **marine** life there can die.

Scientists warn that coral reefs all around the world are in danger. Anything you do to help the environment will help the coral reef survive.

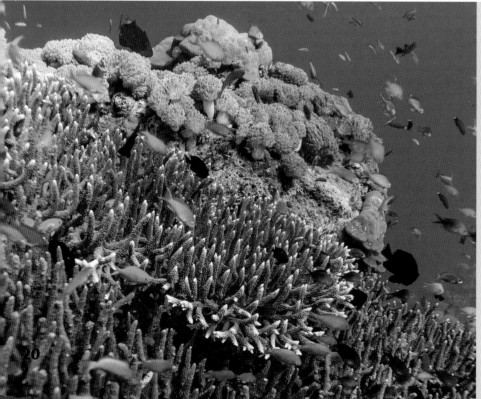

Coral bleaching

Coral bleaching happens when corals turn completely white because of stress. Corals get stressed by increased water temperature or pollution. When stressed, the coral expel the **algae** that live in them and make the coral have colour.

Help the reef by helping the environment!

Recycle

Why? It conserves energy, which will reduce global warming.

Dispose of rubbish properly

Why? Rubbish ends up in the water, where it can harm animals that live around the reef. For example, sea turtles eat jellyfish and can mistake plastic bags in the water for jellyfish.
If they eat the plastic bags, they could die.

Save water

Why? The less water we use, the less wastewater will run back into the oceans.

Talk about the reef

Encourage your friends and family to take care of their homes and gardens by using **biodegradable** chemicals. Non-biodegradable chemicals used in gardens get washed away by rain. Eventually they end up in the sea, where they can harm coral reefs. Biodegradable chemicals break down and do not go into rivers or oceans.

Visit reefs where people are careful not to damage the reef and where they protect reef animals.

Diary of a primary school environmentalist

When our class at school found out about the devastation of the coral reefs, we wanted to help. But we don't live anywhere near a reef. So we decided to organise a day to clean up our local beach.

We organised rubbish bags and gloves. We asked some grown-ups to help us with anything dangerous we might find, like broken glass. We made a big sign to tell people what we were doing.

The day was amazing. We got lots of rubbish from the beach, but more incredible was how many people came past and wanted to help us. One man was so impressed he said that he would donate recycling bins so that people would have a safe place to put rubbish in the future.

In the end we were happy that all the rubbish we picked up that day would not cause harm and that our beach was beautiful again.

Glossary

algae a tiny plant

biodegradable breaks down harmlessly

colonies a large group of the same sort of animal living together

current the strong movement of water

fragile easily broken

habitat a place where a plant or animal naturally lives

inhabitant the animals that live in a place

marine things that are found in or relate to the sea

marine park an area of ocean that is protected from fishing or damage

microscopic smaller than can be seen by the naked eye

polyp a small animal with a fixed base, tentacles and a mouth

scavenger an animal that finds dead or discarded food

scuba self contained underwater breathing apparatus

sieve to get food by straining it out of water

snorkelling swimming with a face mask and a breathing tube

tropical warm areas of the world

zooplankton tiny animals living in the water

Index